Ukulele Picking Tunes

FUN SOLOS TO PLAY

I0804482

by Ondřej Šárek

Flame Maple Concert Ukulele FM-C cover image courtesy of Lanikai Ukuleles.

WWW.MELBAY.COM

Preface

This book presents 47 favorite ukulele picking tunes in traditional gCEA re-entrant tuning. All of the solos are presented in notation and tablature with back-up chords included. The slur markings (hammer-ons and pull-offs) are subjective. Feel free to add or subtract slides, hammer-ons, pull-offs and other effects as you see fit. I use the campanella style extensively in the book. When playing in this style it is best to keep the left-hand fingers on the fingerboard as long as possible so the strings ring to the max, allowing the notes to "flow into one another". Pick up your ukulele, sit back and have fun playing these newly arranged timeless melodies.

Ondřej Šárek

About the Author

Born in 1979. Ondřej Šárek earned a master's degree in Composition at The Janáček Academy of Music and Performing Arts while simultaneously studying Musicology at The Faculty of Arts at Masaryk University in Brno in the Czech Republic. An award-winning participant in several composition competitions, his chamber orchestra, symphonic and choral works are performed internationally. He has also written three mini-operas plus music for film, television, and theater productions.

As a skillful multi-instrumentalist, he devotes his time to playing and composing for piano, guitar, banjo, ukulele, Irish bouzouki, concertina, diatonic accordion, and mandola. He has arranged solo collections for various instruments, many of which have been released by Mel Bay Publications. Ondřej is also one of the leading arrangers of music for the ukulele, an instrument he hopes will regain its former prominence.

Contents

Cumberland Ridge

William Bay

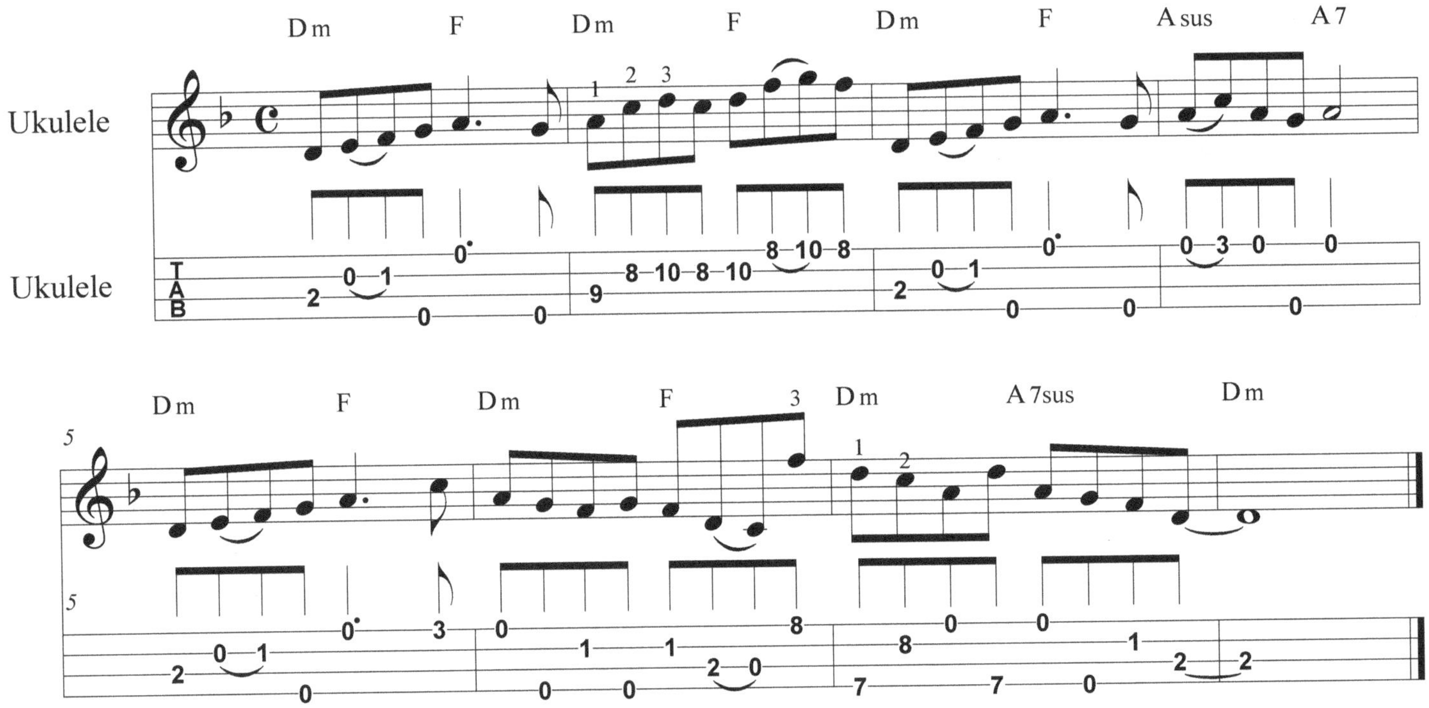

Caleb's Gorge

William Bay

Far from Home

Shetland Islands Reel

The Teetotaller's Reel

Swallowtail Jig

Irish Jig

Morrison's Jig

Irish Jig

The Cuckoo

Southern Mountain Ballad

Barney's Goat

Irish Slip Jig

Red Fox Waltz

The Clergy's Lamentation

O'Carolan

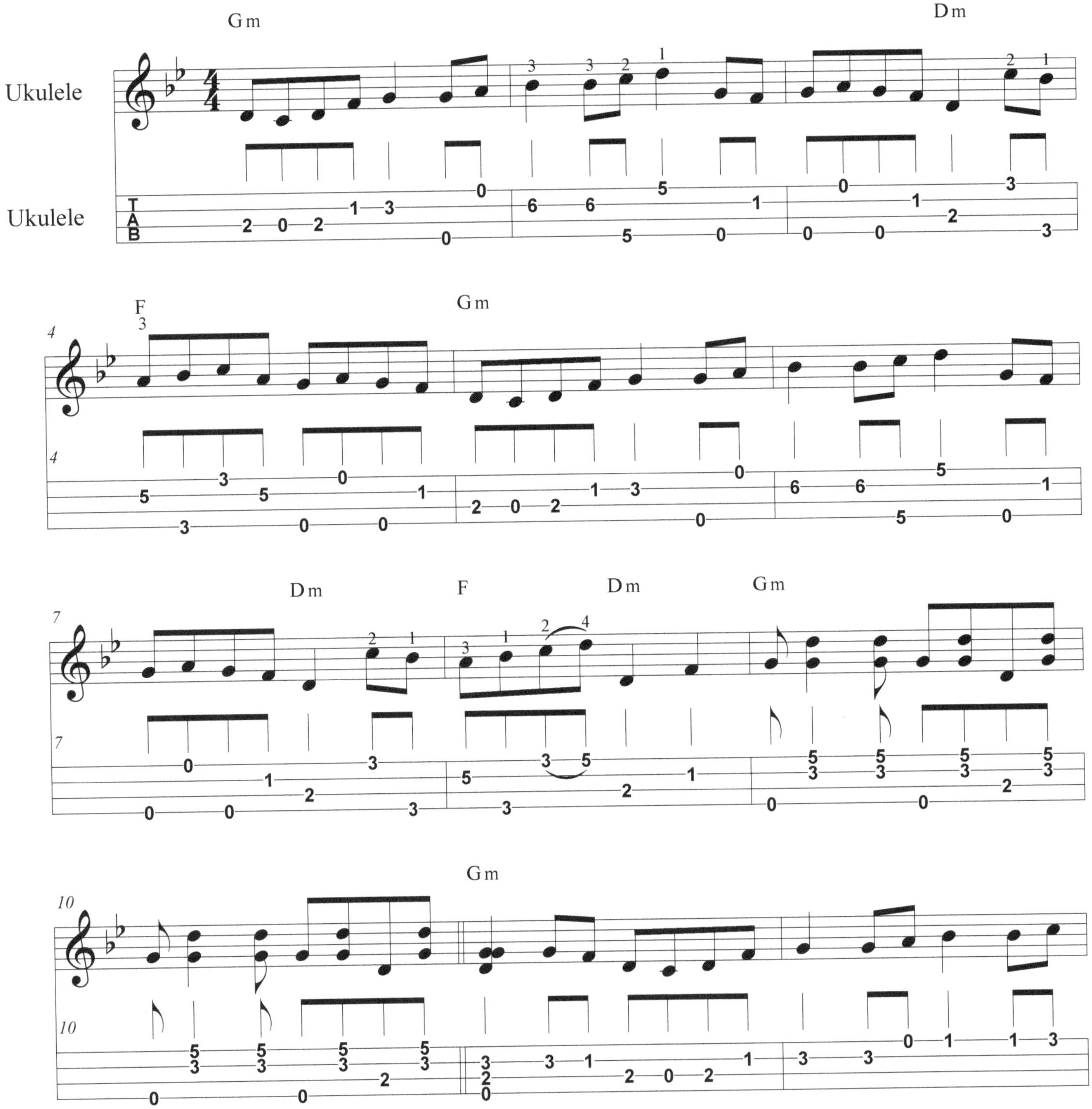

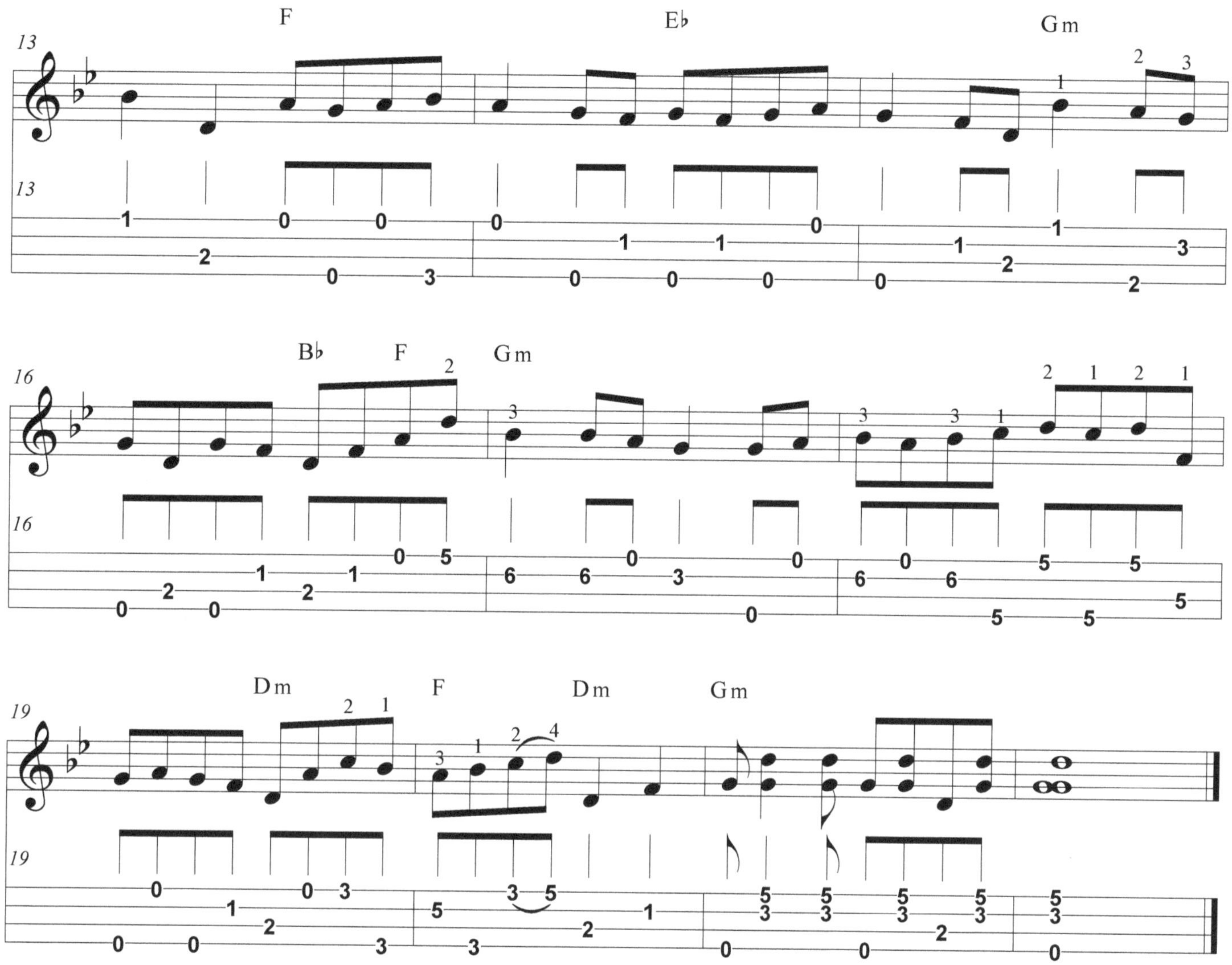
F
E♭
Gm
B♭
F
Gm
Dm
F
Dm
Gm

The Downfall of Paris

Set Dance

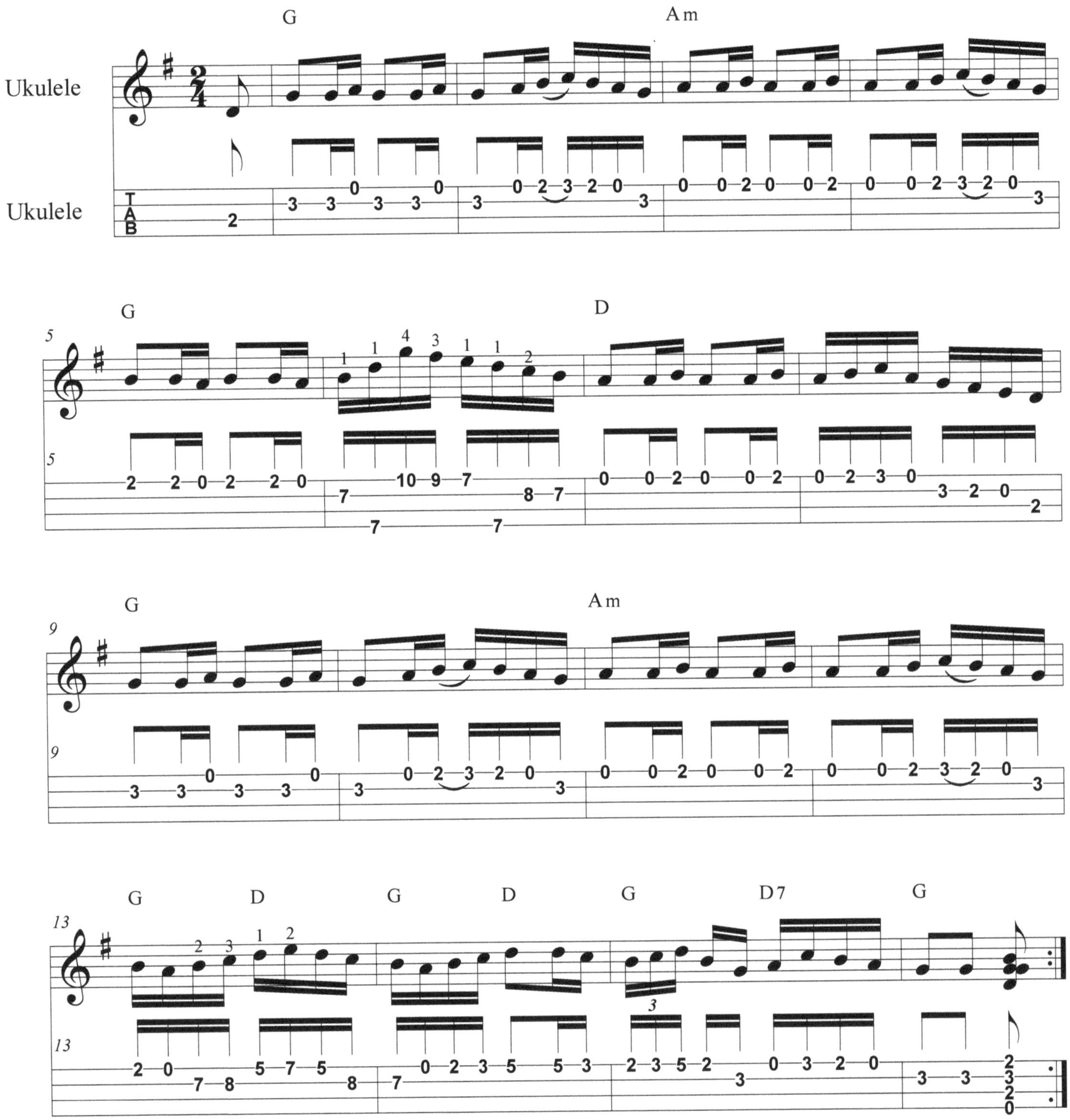

Reel de Lapin

French Canadian

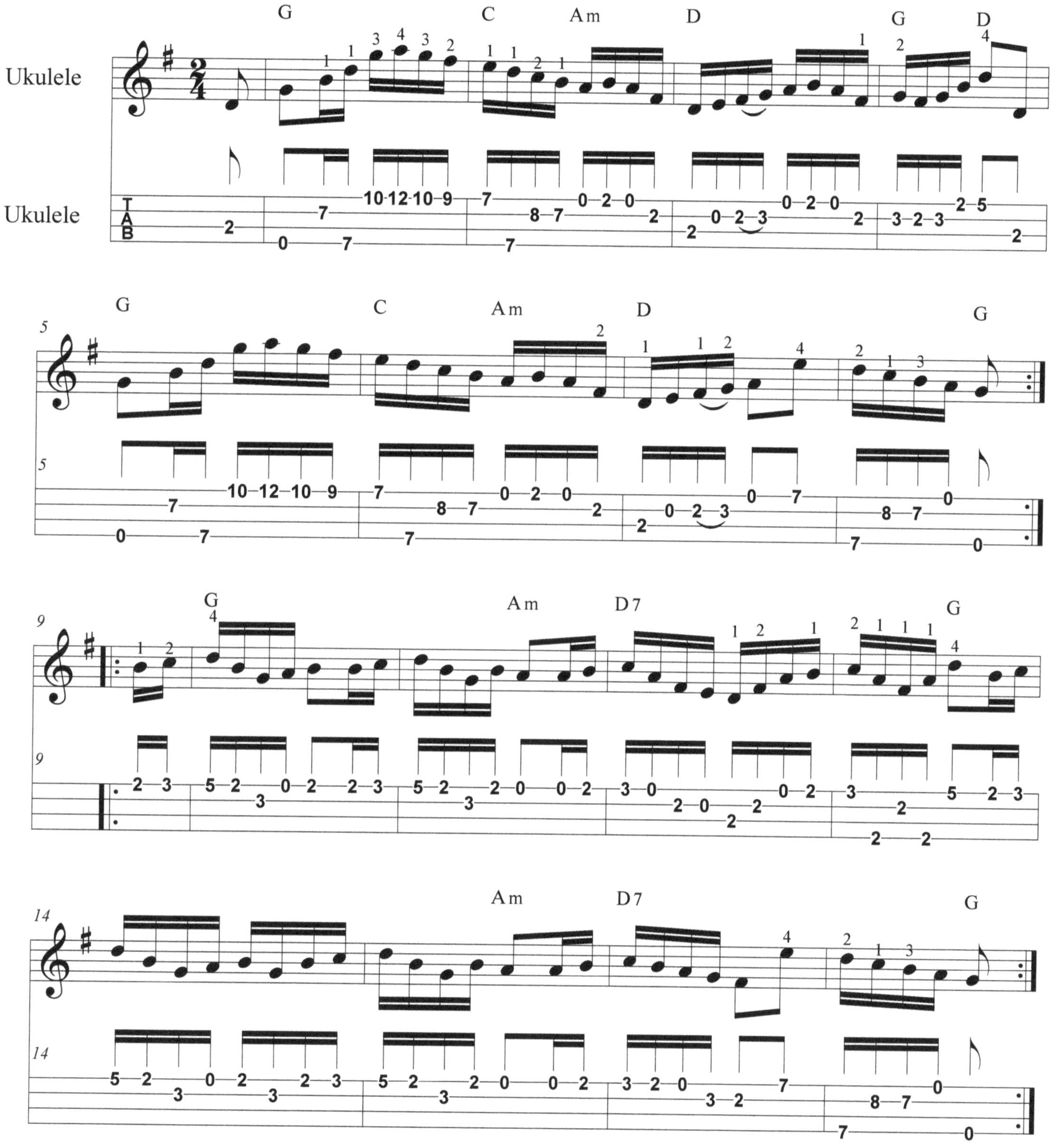

Eleven Mile Canyon

William Bay

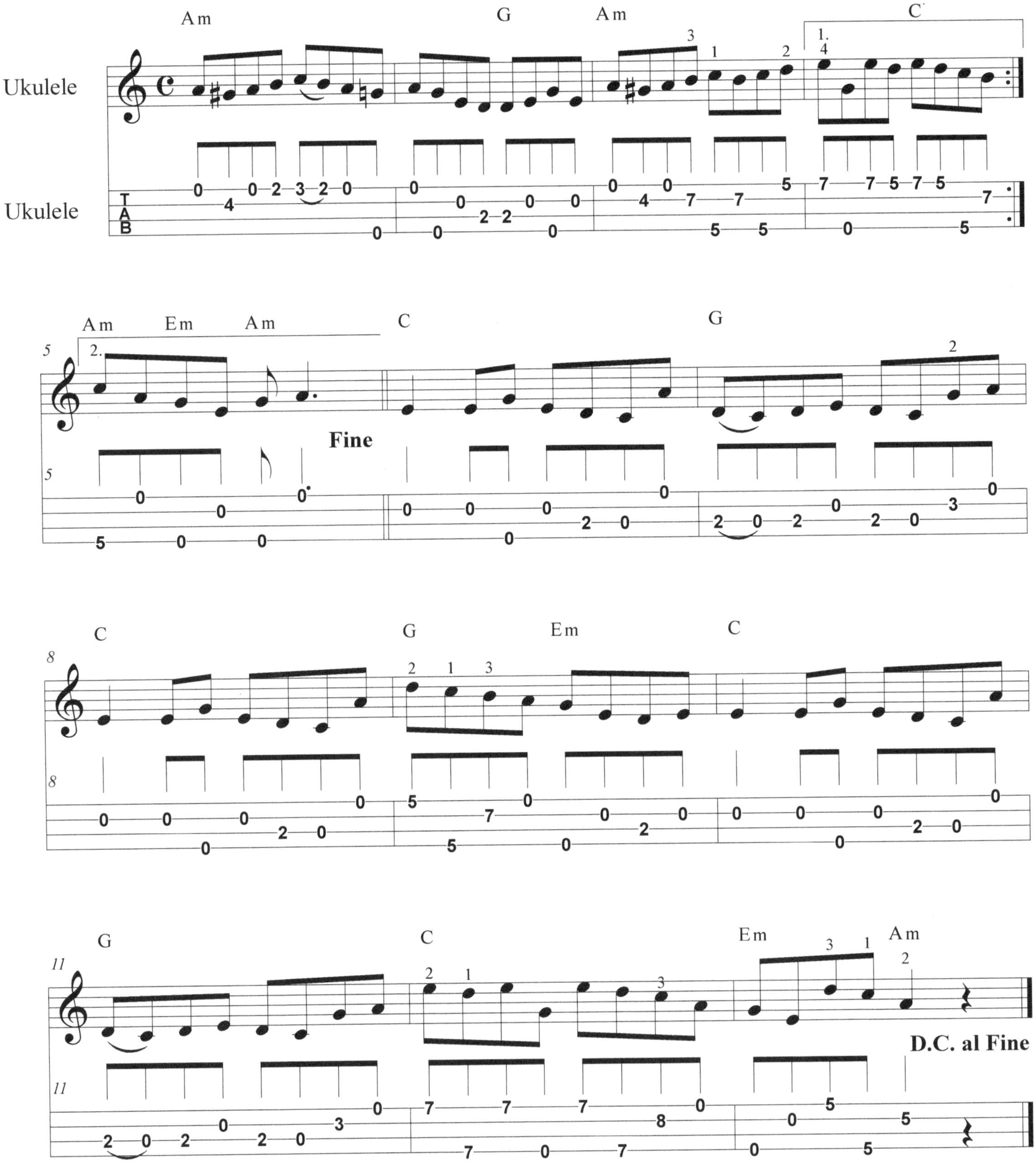

The Burning of the Piper's Hut

Scottish March

Young McGoldrick

William Bay

Jackson's Jig

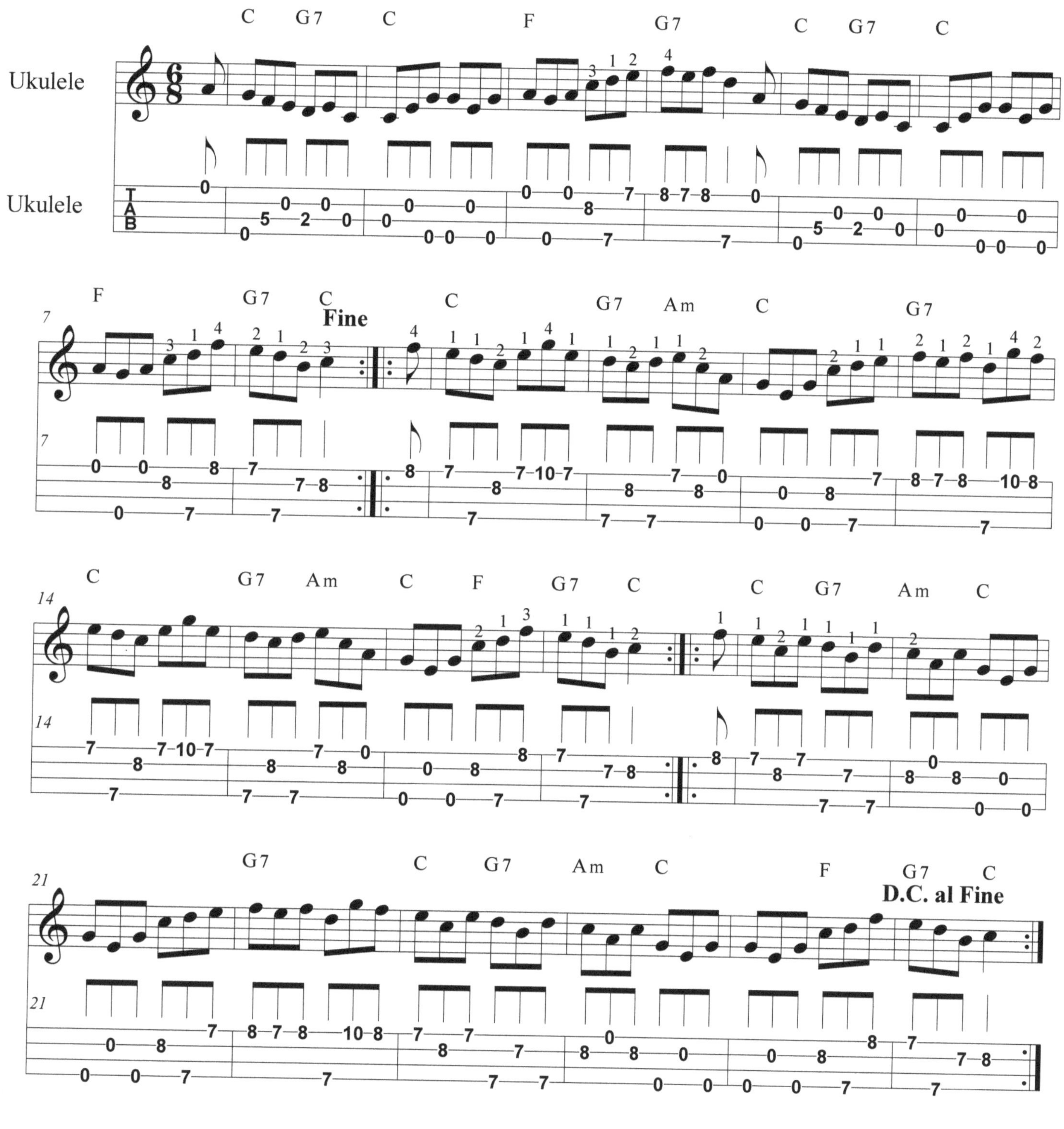

Little House 'Round the Corner

Irish Jig

Missouri Mud

Fiddle Tune

Whiskey Before Breakfast

Neapolitan Threshers

Jig

Eighth of January

Harvest Moon Strathspey

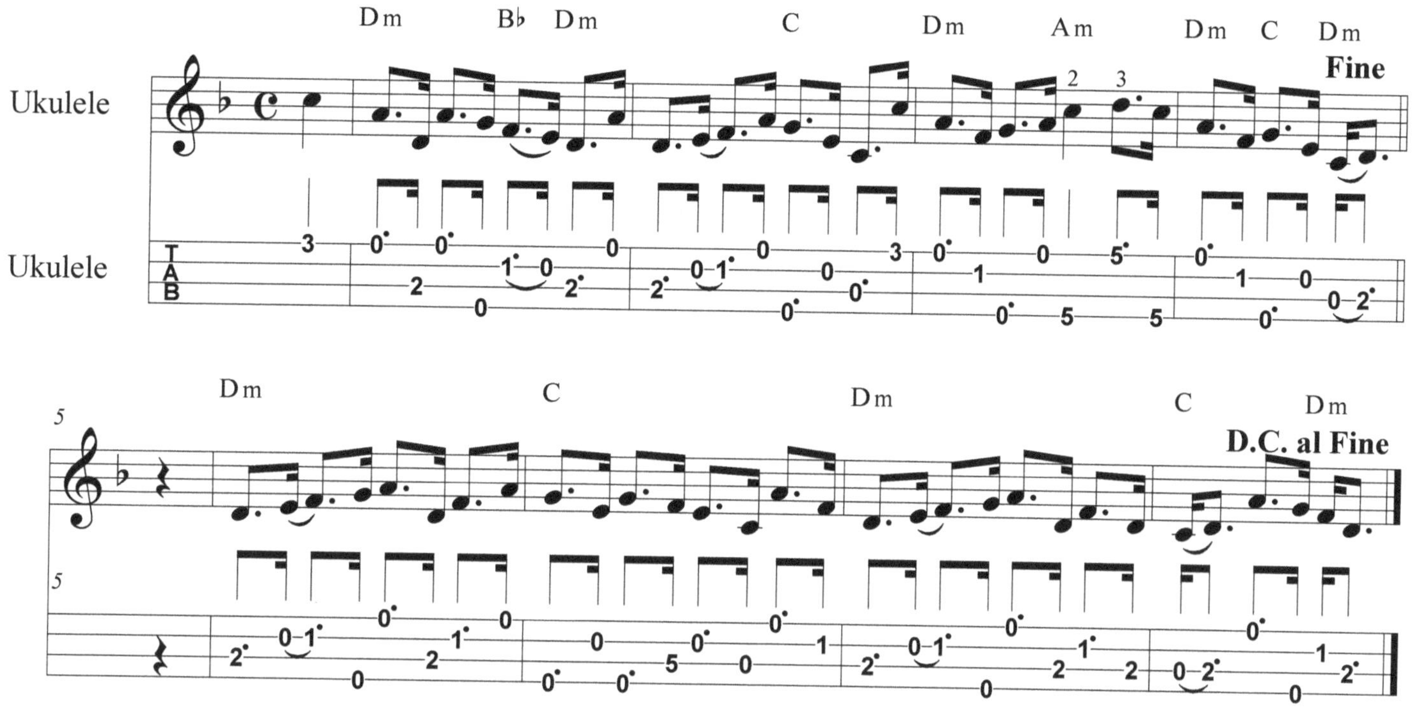

Buttermilk Jig

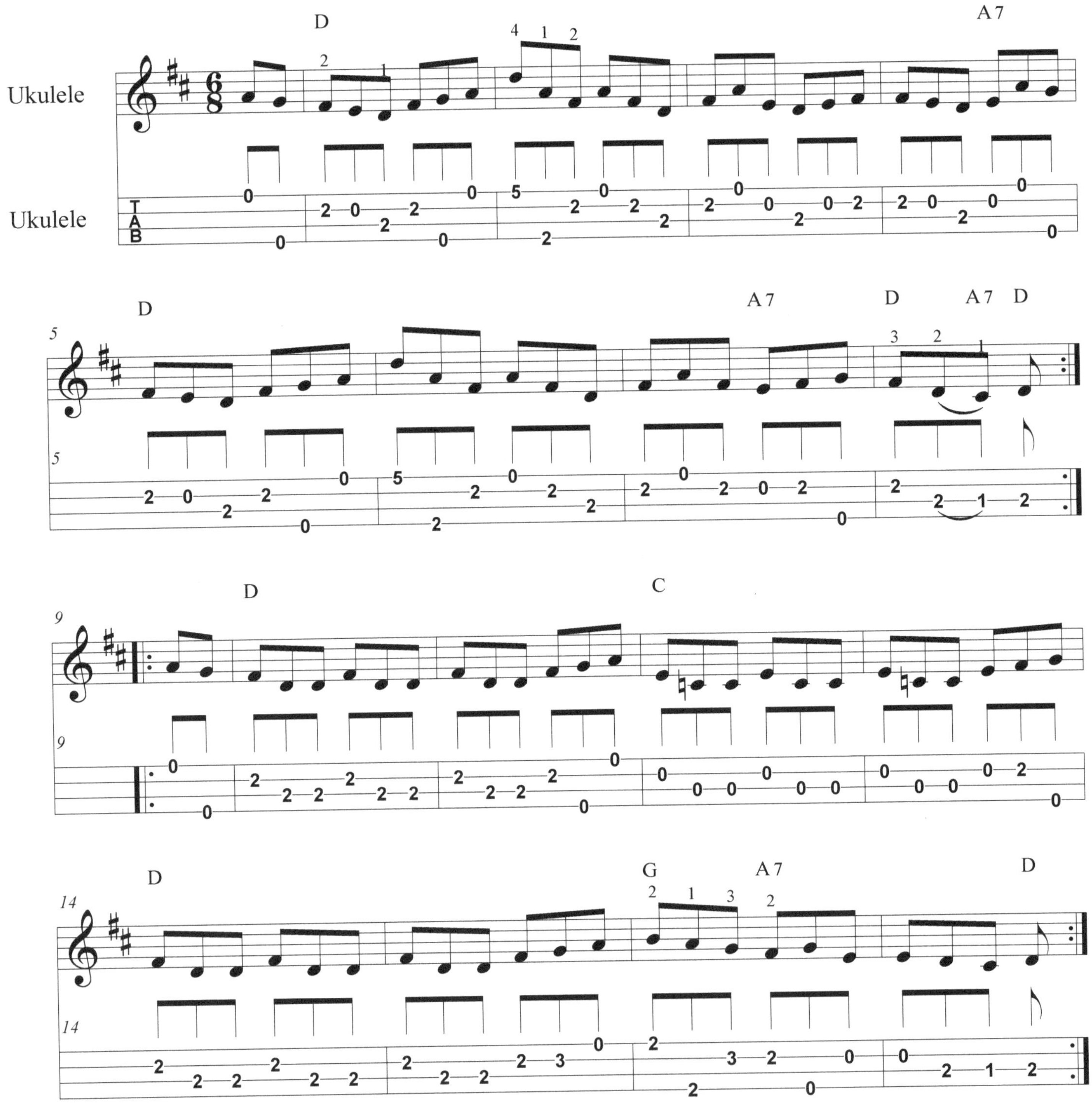

An Comhra Donn

Hornpipe

National Lancer's Hornpipe

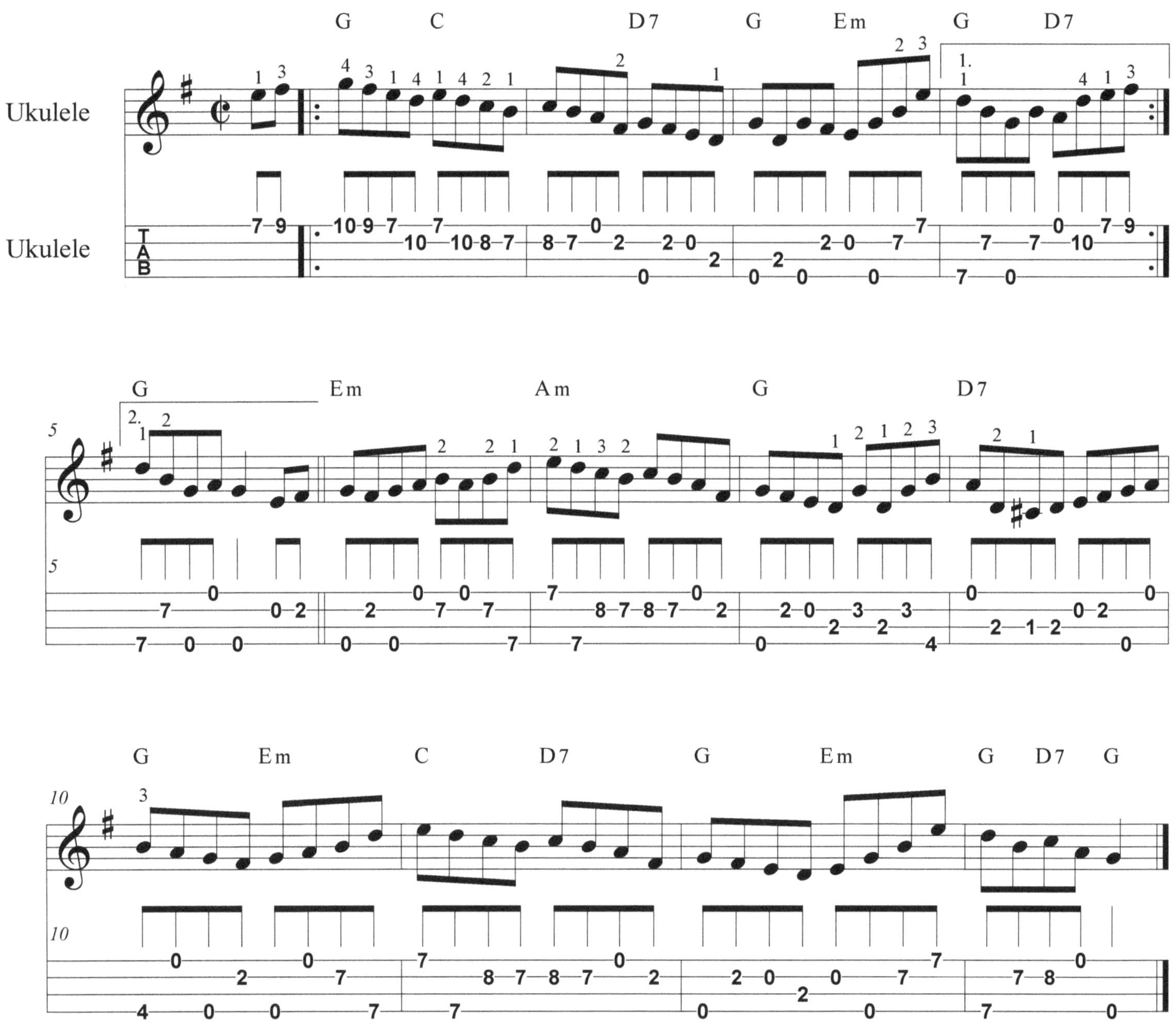

Brighton Beach

William Bay

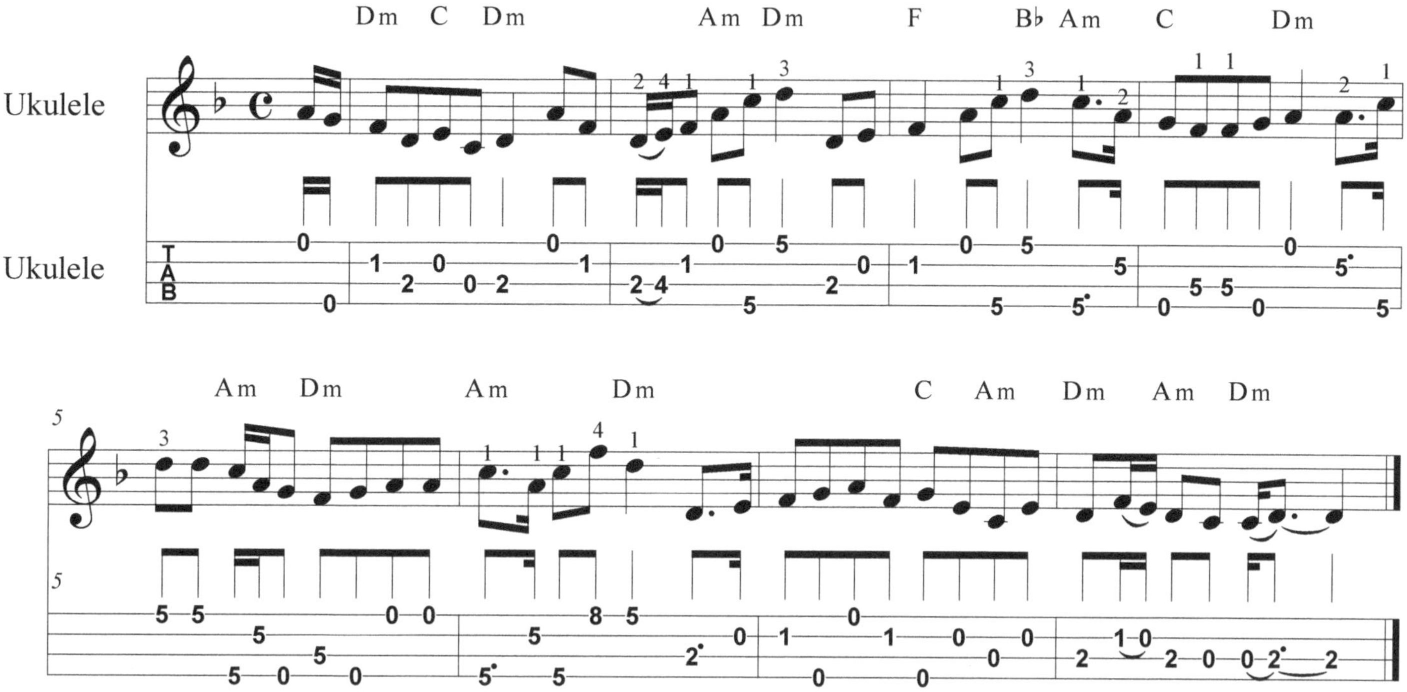

Green Fields of America

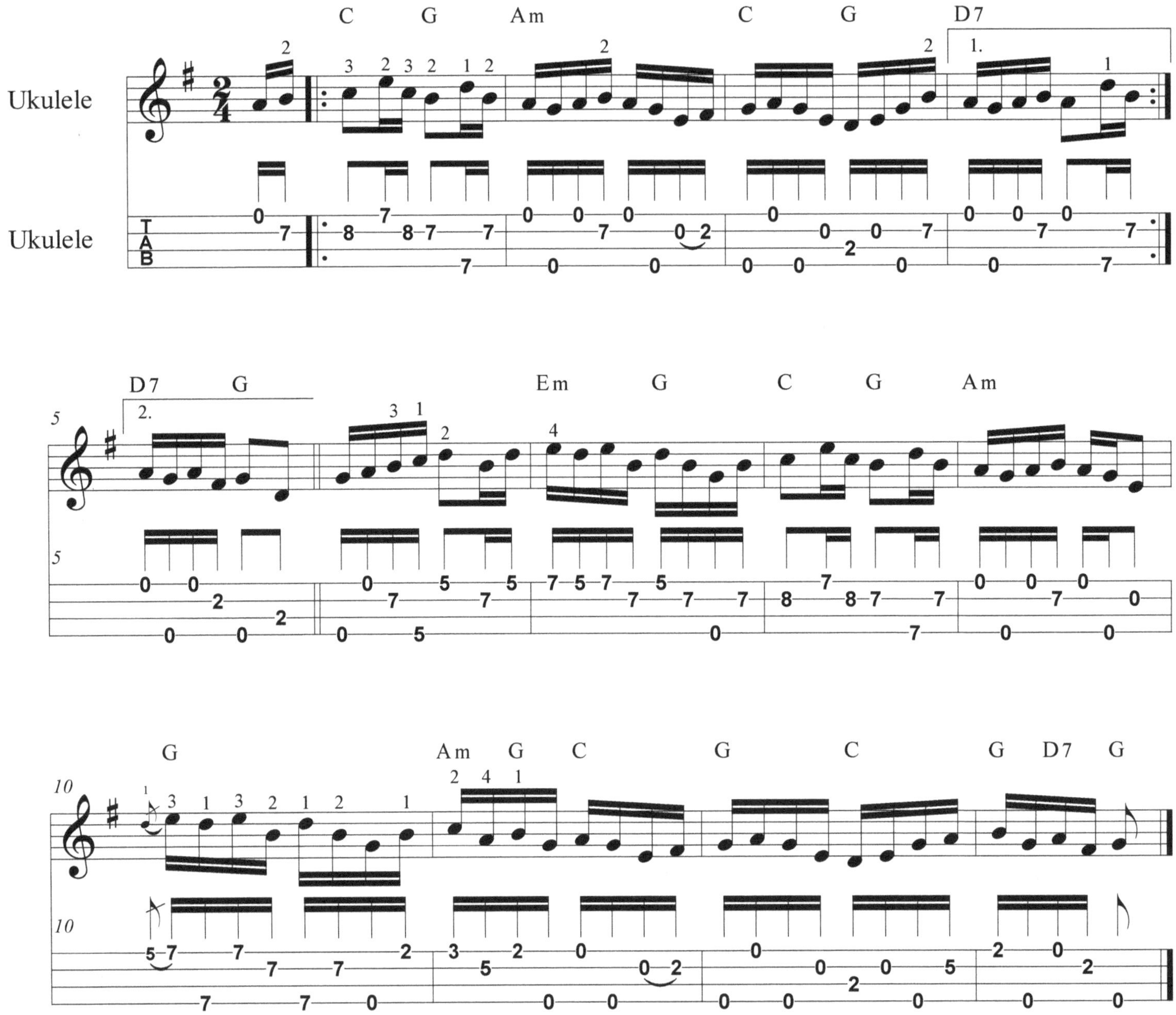

St. Clair's Hornpipe

Star of Bethlehem

Bennett's Favorite Reel

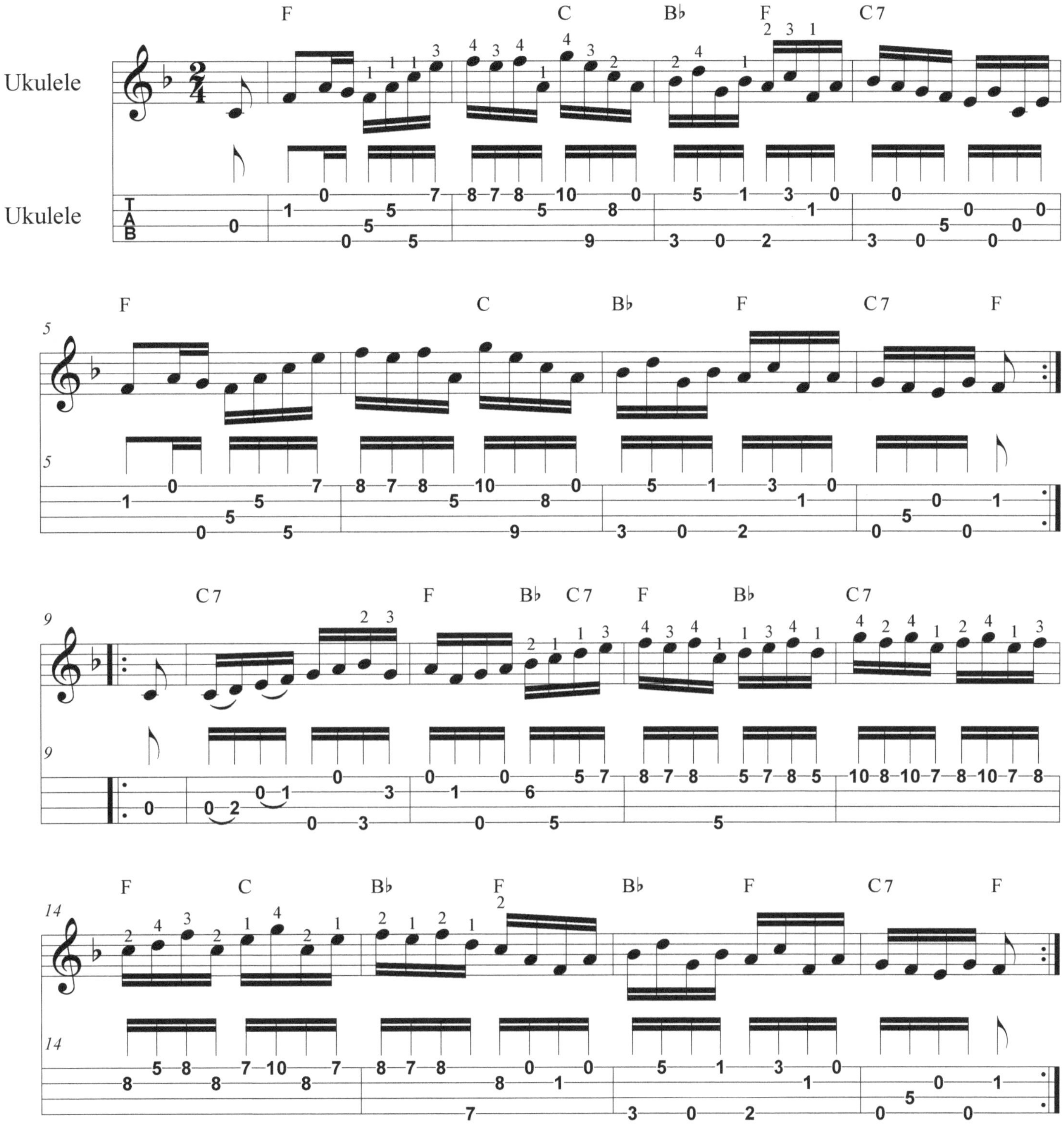

Ivy Leaf Reel

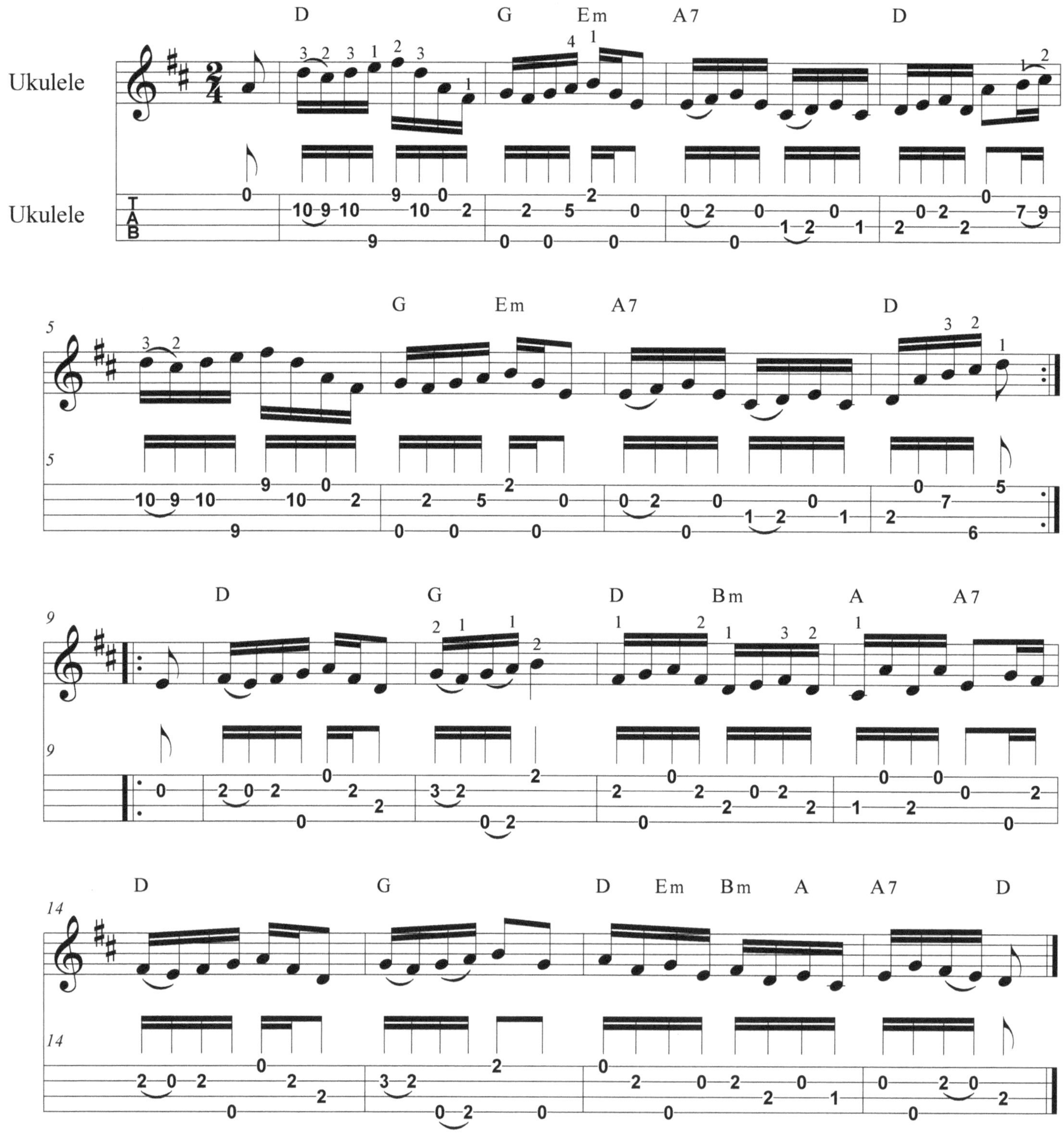

St. Anne's Reel

Gladiator Reel

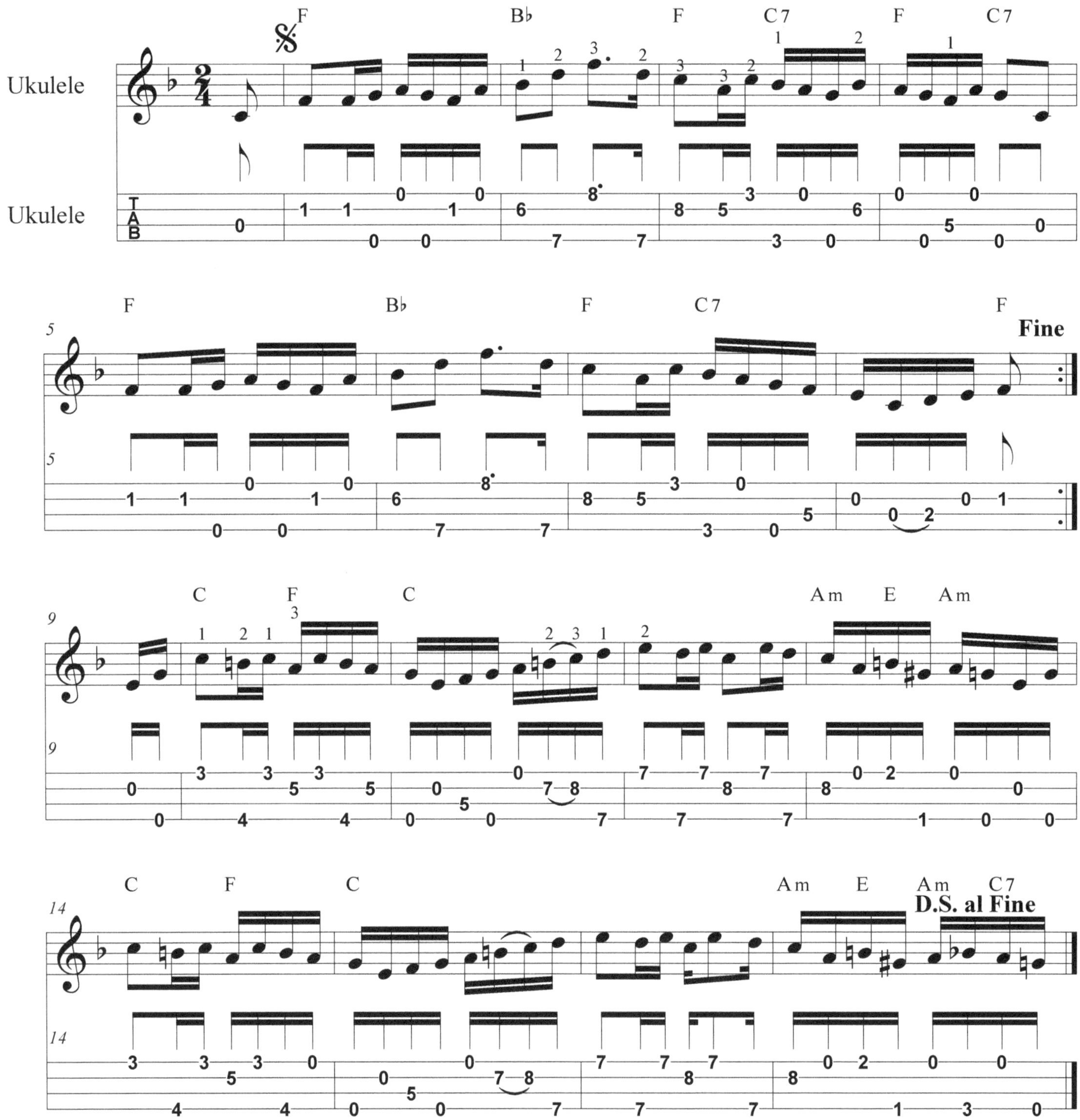

Luckie Bawdin's Reel

Scottish

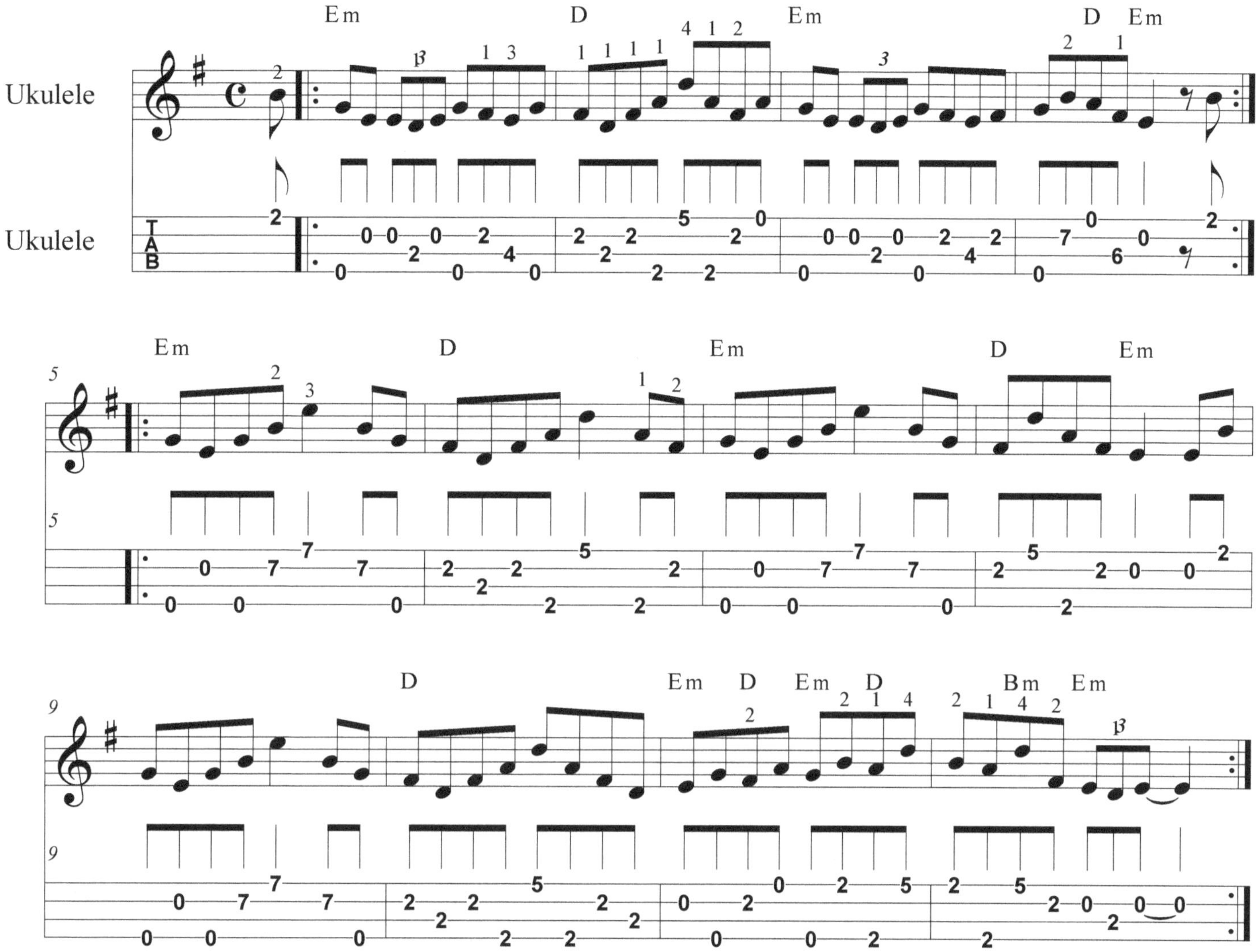

Witch of the Wave Reel

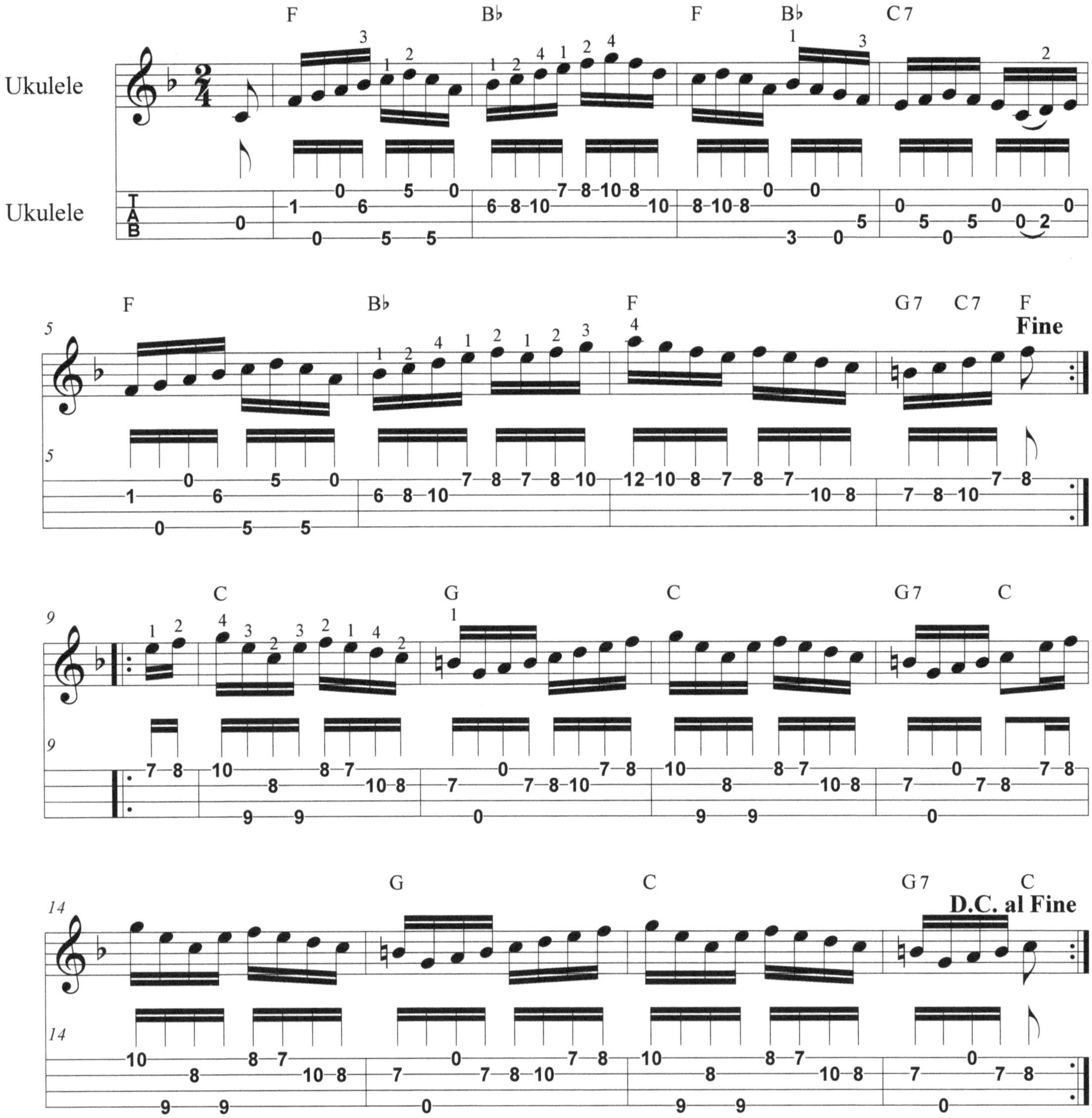

North Sea

William Bay

Red Haired Boy

Mere Point

William Bay

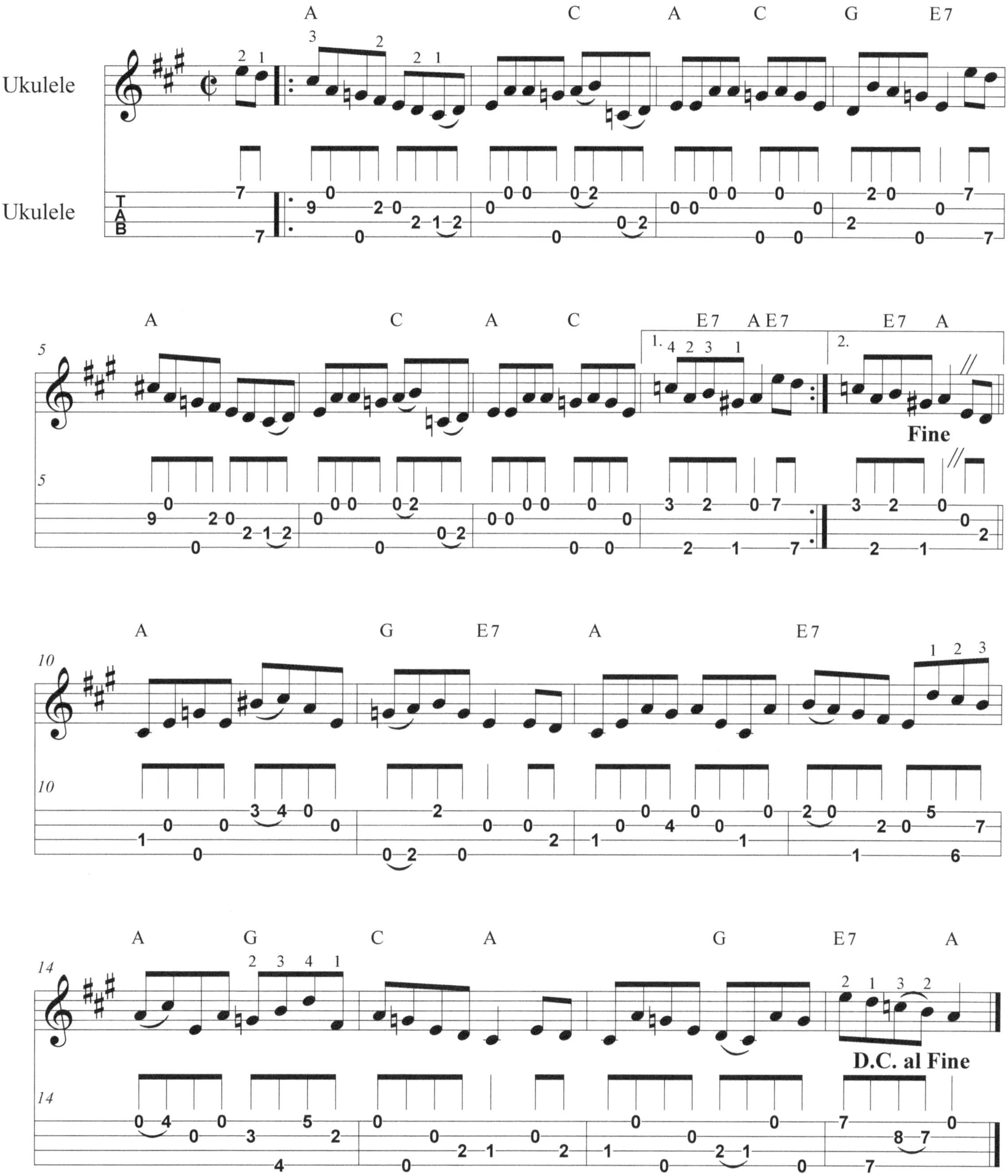

Blackberry Blossom

Days of 'Lang Syne

Scottish

Wilson's Hornpipe

G7
C
F
C
G7
F
G7
C
1.
C
2.

Carolan's Draught

O'Carolan

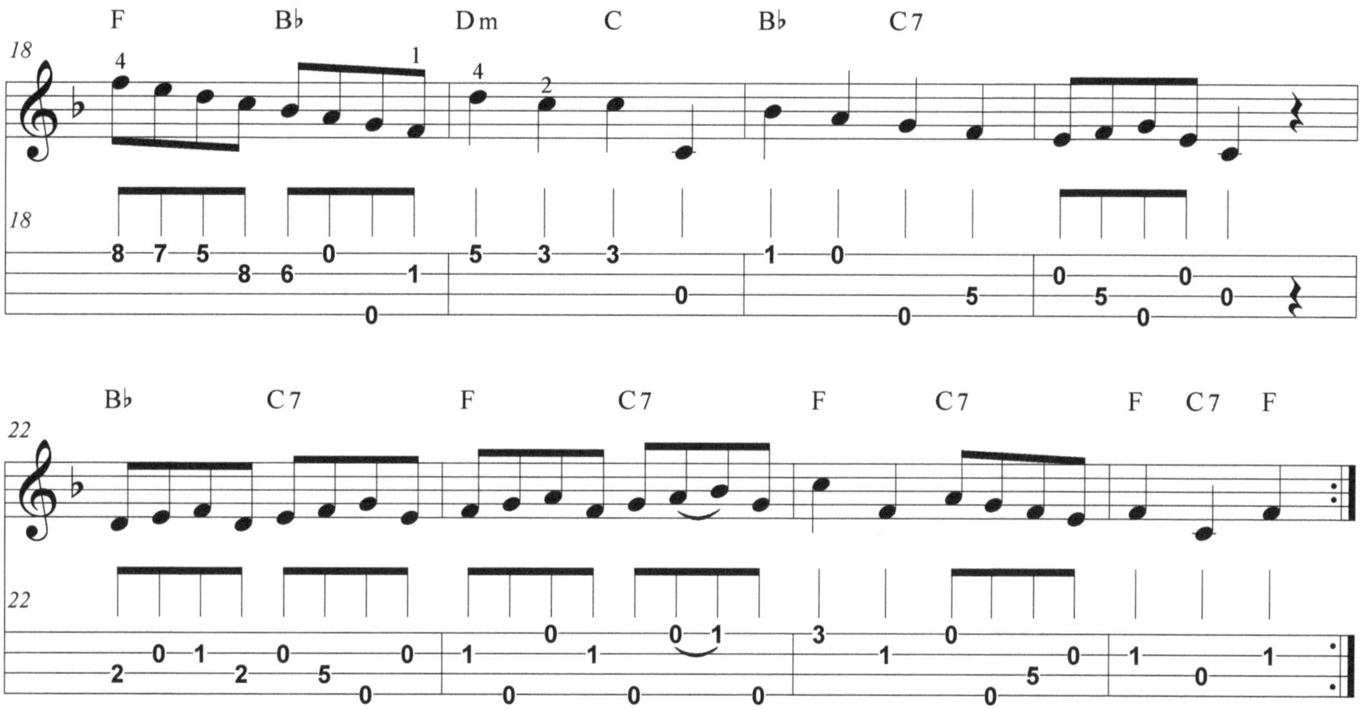
F Bb Dm C Bb C7
Bb C7 F C7 F C7 F C7 F

Brush Creek

William Bay

The Rights of Man

The Unfortunate Rake

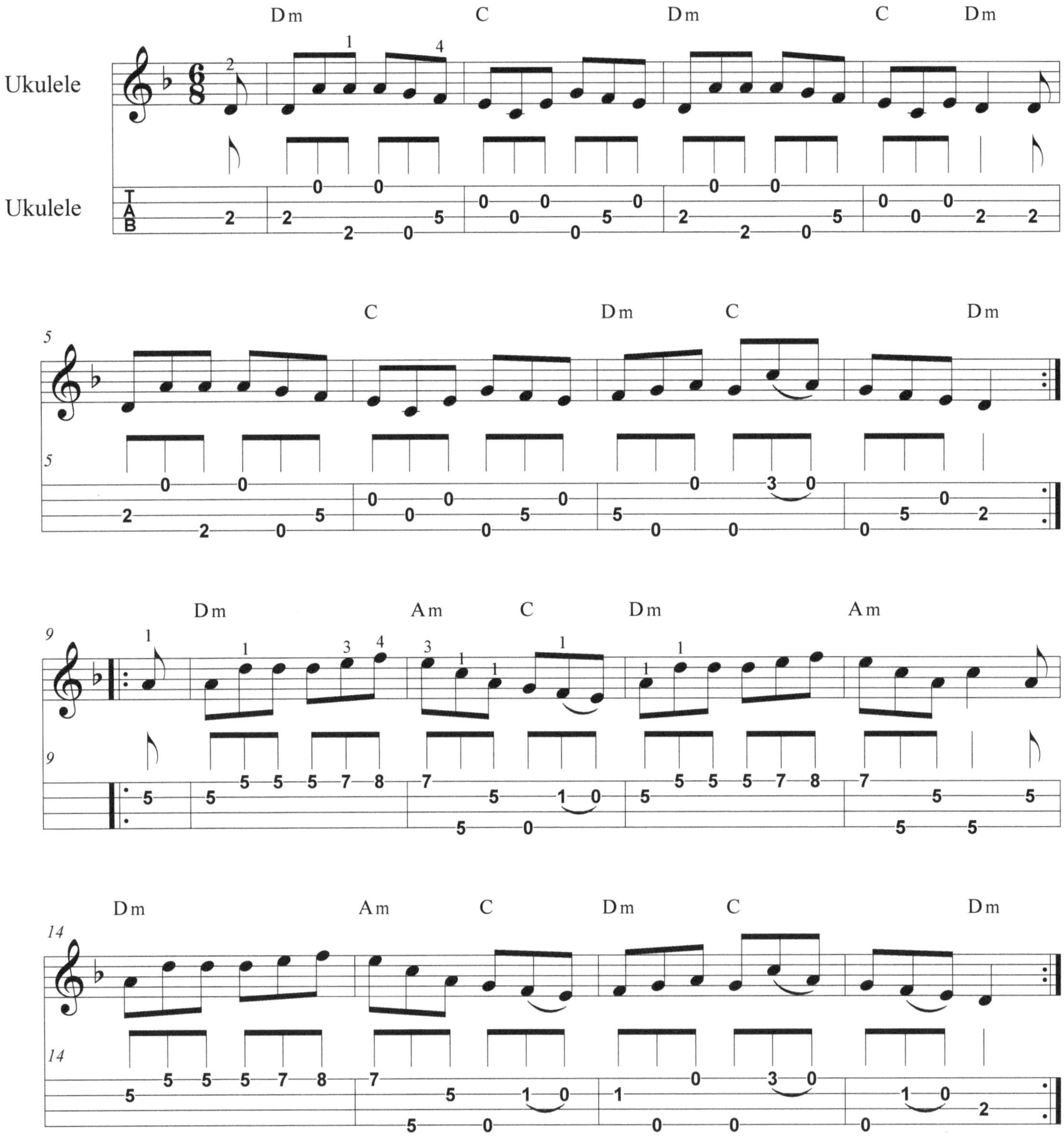

Shannon's Well

William Bay

Lark in the Morning

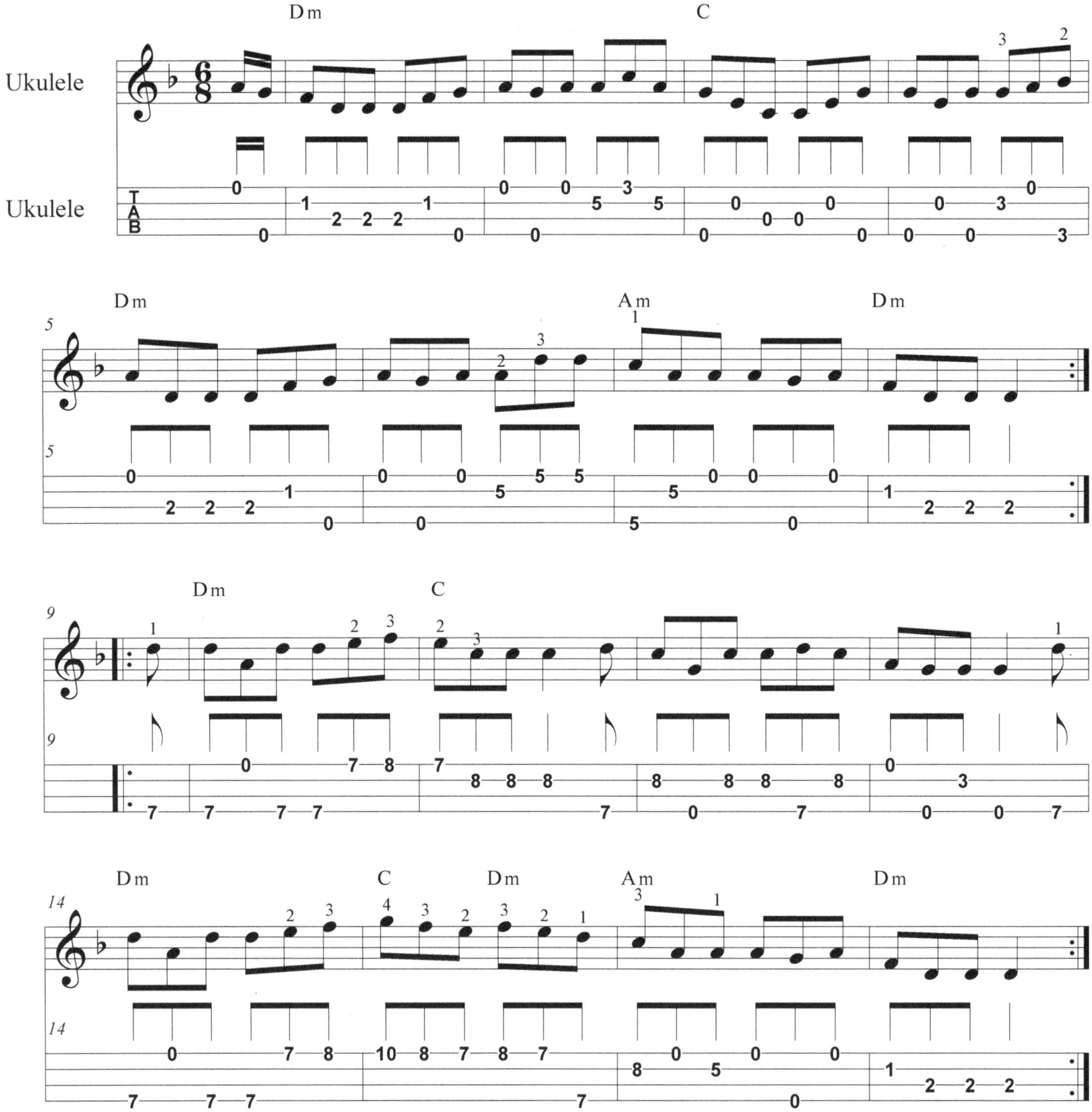